Meditation

A Comprehensive And Systematic Manual For
Cultivating Inner Serenity And Leading A Life Free From
Stress

*(An Effective Approach For Novices To Effortlessly
Alleviate Stress And Cultivate Inner Peace Through
Mindfulness)*

Marc-Andre Thiessen

TABLE OF CONTENT

What Is Meditation?.. 1

The Art Of Meditation: A Concise Introduction........23

Meditation - An All-Encompassing Phenomenon...38

What Are The Advantages Of Utilizing Hypnosis? .68

The Psychosocial Development Across The Lifespan 78

Meditation And Success 91

Meditation..104

Following Your Breath..118

The Various Strata Of Our Being..................................127

Posture For Meditation: A 7-Step Guide...................139

An Analysis Of The Fundamental Aspects Of Meditation: The Elements Of Who, What, Where, When, Why, With, And How 151

What Is Meditation?

Meditation is a widely recognized practice, yet there remains a need for a more profound understanding of its essence. Despite its widespread popularity, only a minority possess comprehensive knowledge about its nature. There are numerous misconceptions surrounding the practice of meditation. Several aspects of meditation involve focusing solely on a designated object and refraining from any other thoughts. Some individuals may perceive it as a creative endeavor that provides tranquility. Certain individuals believe that a particular form of physical activity is necessary in order to bring about a state of tranquility for both the body and the mind. One of the most prevalent falsehoods is the belief that it is obligatory to maintain silence, engage in deep reflection, and achieve mental clarity.

Indeed, meditation can be described as the state of cognitive presence devoid of active thinking. Of attaining knowledge about one's conscious experiences. The coordinated effort of acknowledging one's thoughts, emotions, and bodily condition. There exist numerous methods to engage in meditation, yet they all share the common objective of attaining a state of uncluttered consciousness.

Every single method of meditation is unified in its purpose, which is to attain personal tranquility through a state of serene passivity combined with unwavering attentiveness. The brain's oscillations decelerate while maintaining consciousness of the environment, entering a state of relaxation combined with vigilance. An aura of tranquility and vigilance.

Why Practice Meditation?

Meditation is considered to be one of the most efficacious methods for alleviating stress. Despite the cultivation and examination of alternative stress reduction strategies, the evidence suggests that none are as efficacious as the practice of meditation. Extensive research has been undertaken to ascertain the efficacy and potential health benefits of meditation.

A research conducted in the United States has demonstrated that the implementation of a brief program focusing on behavioral modification techniques, which incorporates meditation, resulted in a notable decrease in doctor visits over a period of six months and sustained the reduction for an additional six-month period.

There are a multitude of compelling reasons to engage in meditation, as it offers a plethora of health advantages, enhances one's capacity for contentment and problem-solving, fosters improved concentration and memory, fortifies individuals against the burdensome pressures found both in professional and personal domains, effectively diminishing anxiety and stress levels, and ultimately enhances performance in various athletic pursuits, among a host of other notable benefits.

Benefits of Meditation

Meditation proves efficacious in combating stress and profoundly enhances both mental and physical well-being, thereby enhancing overall quality of life. To such an extent that it may facilitate a reduction in healthcare expenditures.

Through diligent practice, the act of meditation will ultimately be accomplished with ease. Engaging in genuine meditation facilitates the redirection of your attention towards the present moment, allowing you to refrain from fixating on past experiences or uncertain future events.

Meditation is versatile. Insufficient, limited evidence exists to establish the superiority of one technique over another. Each individual possesses their own unique nature and displays varying responses to the diverse forms of meditation available. The allure of meditation lies in the abundant options available to engage in this practice. By selecting a technique that resonates with you and maintaining a dedicated approach, the positive outcomes can be obtained irrespective of the chosen method.

While the primary objective of meditation does not typically involve seeking relaxation, it frequently leads to a notable sense of calm as a significant outcome. Research findings indicate that meditation yields a multitude of advantageous outcomes. The benefits include:

- Enhanced Circulation of Blood

- Reduce arterial pressure

- Reduced sweating • Decreased perspiration • Lowered amount of sweat production • Diminished sweat excretion

- Reduction in heart rate

- Reduced rate of respiration

- Reduction in Cortisol Levels in the Bloodstream

- Reduced levels of anxiety

- Reduced levels of stress

- Increased sense of overall well-being • Heightened feelings of wellness • Enhanced emotional state • Greater sense of positivity and contentment

- Enhanced relaxation experience • Heightened state of relaxation • Profoundly relaxed state • Increased level of relaxation • Attainment of deeper relaxation levels

The Impact of Meditation on the Brain

Extensive medical research has yielded evidence suggesting that meditation has a substantial impact on the augmentation of gray matter in the brain, specifically in regions linked to motor coordination, cognitive retention, sensory processing, affective experience, and verbal communication.

According to research undertaken by the Laboratory for the Neuroscientific Investigation of Meditation and Mind

Body Medicine at Massachusetts General Hospital, it was observed that engaging in a daily meditation practice for a minimum of 30 minutes over a span of 8 weeks resulted in a notable augmentation of gray matter density in the hippocampus. This corresponds to the cognitive regions of our brain that are tied to the processes of memory and learning.

Brain scans conducted on the participants unveiled a significant decrease in gray matter within the amygdala, a neural region associated with stress and anxiety. The research findings indicate that meditation has been found to be associated with a reduction in amygdala density, as well as a decrease in reactivity to emotionally evocative images as supported by available evidence.

The Happiness Factor

Mediation contributes significantly to the enhancement of quality of life through various means. It offers more happiness, it provides us a way to see things more clearly, and there are clear health benefits. The individual with a well-honed ability in meditation exudes an aura of serenity and extends it to those around them.

Vipassana is commonly referred to as mindful meditation in its traditional context. It serves as the core foundation of meditation within the Buddhist community, and has garnered greater recognition and adherence across

Southeast Asian regions. It places a strong emphasis on the cultivation of mindfulness, subsequently fostering heightened self-awareness that permeates various facets of an individual's everyday life. There are individuals who ascribe it to the art of existence. It entails a profound experience of self-discovery, a departure from a state of mindless routine, a return to the present moment, and a realization of the potential to engage in wiser, more compassionate, and more fulfilling ways of existence.

Effective Techniques for Enhancing Cognitive Abilities through Meditation

Utilizing any form of meditation methodology on a consistent basis, provided that it is performed daily, can serve the objective of enhancing cognitive abilities. Indeed, it is imperative that the meditation be of utmost quality, with wholehearted immersion into the meditative state, in order for it to yield beneficial effects on the brain. Allow me to provide some guidance on how to accomplish that:

Label your thoughts. When a thought arises that diverts your attention from the central objective, assign it a label. This will serve as an indication to the mind that you are indeed acknowledging the occurrence of drifting, yet you are determined to prevent it from wholly diverting you from the state of meditation. A few illustrations of labels could include designations such as "professional," "personal," "educational," and "imaginary" cogitations.

Don't judge yourself. Whenever you find yourself prolonging your train of thought rather than engaging in meditation, refrain from succumbing to the notion that you lack proficiency in meditation or that you are not predisposed to meditative practice. These will greatly impede the entire process. Rather, consider the notion that meditation is accessible to all individuals, particularly yourself. Subsequently, promptly redirect your undivided attention towards the primary subject of your concentration.

Incorporate the practice of meditation into your routine whenever possible. It is not imperative for one to assume a seated position in order to engage in meditation. One can perform this task at any given moment while occupied with mundane activities like cleaning the vehicle or engaging in regular household chores. You are able to engage in this activity at any point in time when you experience emotional distress. Inhale and attentively witness the stream of your thoughts as if you were suspended above your own consciousness, engaging in the act of perusing the mental constructs of a separate individual. Take periodic breaks of two minutes to engage in deep breathing exercises.

Meditation enables individuals to cultivate the ability to concentrate on a single designated focal point at a given moment. This exercise enhances cognitive capacity, thereby facilitating the ability to concentrate on other significant pursuits, such as professional obligations and innovative thinking. Engaging in the practice of meditation can likewise enhance your meta-cognitive abilities, a fundamental component of comprehensive intellectual capacity.

Helpful Hints

Make an effort to incorporate your meditation sessions into your daily schedule, ensuring that you are consistently mindful of the times designated for rejuvenating your own energies. Through meticulous scheduling of your meditation sessions, you are fostering the transformation of meditation into a constructive routine. Another advantage is that acquaintances, relatives, and co-workers will be informed of your unavailability during this period.

Do not confine regulated respiration solely to the practice of meditation; instead, whenever you experience sensations of anxiety, stress, or anger, allocate a few moments to simply engage in the act of deep breathing. Your consciousness will be conditioned to perceive that specific pattern of respiration as an opportunity to decelerate your pulse and stabilize your thoughts; eventually, this response will become an innate reflex.

Prior to commencing your meditation practice, make an effort to unwind and release tension from your muscles. If you experience heightened levels of tension, engage in a brief period of stretching exercises as a means to alleviate muscular tightness. You wouldn't desire your meditation to be disrupted by the contraction of muscles.

Please bear in mind that achieving the ability to prevent one's mind from drifting during meditation requires a significant amount of dedicated practice over an extended period. Do not permit yourself to become frustrated by it. Redirect your efforts and perseveringly proceed.

Please bear in mind that meditation serves the purpose of cultivating overall wellness of one's mind, body, and spirit, and preserving such state of being. Look forward to it. When experiencing the burdens of life, it may be perceived that meditation is an arduous task. However, it is precisely in such moments that one must steadfastly surmount this obstacle, as an untreated mind will progressively deteriorate over time. Engaging in positive meditation will effectively eliminate this hurdle within a brief period.

Make an effort to establish a regular connection with your body either on a weekly or monthly basis. Regularly engage in the Getting to know your body exercise to maintain constant awareness of any physical changes that may be transpiring within your being.

Select the most optimal time of day to engage in meditation. The morning is an opportune period that fosters a favorable commencement of the day, yet its feasibility is not always viable. If it becomes necessary for you to wake up one hour earlier in order to accommodate your meditation practice, it may be advantageous in spite of the potential consequence of experiencing fatigue at an earlier hour in the evening. Ensure that your daily schedule is structured in a manner that readily accommodates the allocated time for your meditation practice. If necessary, pursue your tasks during the evening hours while considering what timing suits you best.

Incorporating one's family members into the practice of meditation is frequently recommended. For individuals leading highly occupied lifestyles, this can prove to be a highly effective means of cherishing family moments or engaging in quality interactions with a significant other. Despite the absence of verbal communication, both individuals will nonetheless be attuning themselves to the collective energies of the universe, forging a profound connection at an entirely distinct plane. Engaging in collective meditation can serve as a valuable mechanism to foster greater bonds among individuals.

If you intend to incorporate children into your meditation regimen, it is important to acknowledge that a child's mind possesses a significantly limited capacity for sustained focus. If your child expresses interest in participating, it is advisable to initially keep their meditation sessions brief and adjust them according to their age and attention span.

Depending on their age, children may have a greater propensity for engaging in focus-oriented meditation practices. Instead of providing a candle, present them with a receptacle of water accompanied by water-based paints. A small quantity of pigmented paint, agitated within water, can manifest captivating forms and designs. Kindly request their perusal and identification of any discernible imagery present. Moreover, this approach significantly contributes to fostering the child's imaginative capabilities.

Incorporating meditation into a child's nighttime regimen can aptly complement their bedroom routine. It will help ease their mental activity and induce a state of relaxation, ensuring a deep and rejuvenating sleep followed by a refreshed awakening. It is important to exercise caution and refrain from exerting undue pressure when introducing meditation to children, as not all of them may be amenable to it or possess the necessary patience. If individuals express a desire to participate, kindly embrace and foster their involvement; however, if they opt not to do so, it is prudent to graciously relinquish any expectations or pursuits related to their engagement.

The Art Of Meditation: A Concise Introduction

You have chosen to engage with this book due to your deep concern for the welfare and equilibrium of your mental and emotional faculties. It is likely that you have encountered or been informed of the advantageous characteristics of meditation, particularly its efficacy in combating stress and anxiety, as well as its potential to enhance your general state of serenity and contentment.

This chapter serves as a succinct overview for acquainting you with the concept of meditation, ensuring that you attain a comprehensive understanding of its essence.

Meditation Explained in Layman's Terms

A concise explication of meditation in formal discourse reads as follows: "Meditation is best understood as a diligent pursuit of attentiveness, employing techniques such as concentration, mindfulness, and awareness to cultivate the mind's unwavering focus on a specific object or topic." From an etymological standpoint, the term signifies the act of engaging in contemplation, reflection, or deep consideration.

Upon further examination of this definition, we can ascertain the subsequent notion: "due to the fact that meditation involves the deliberate cultivation of conscious attentiveness or mindfulness, it should not be perceived as mere action, the absence of thought, or an exercise in exerting dominance over the mind."

It is of utmost significance that you comprehend and assimilate this differentiation, as meditation, in contrast to commonly held beliefs, does not require one to exert control over the mind or regulate the stream of thoughts. Rather, meditation simply requires you to cultivate intentional consciousness towards a specific object or concept, which can encompass a wide range of possibilities such as the mind's characteristics, the breath, an illuminated candle, the physical body, a plant, walking motions, a mental image, certain phrases, and more.

Meditation has the ability to be conducted in both formal and informal settings. Formal meditation entails precisely allocating time to engage in concentrated mental attention on a specified object or aspect over a predetermined period, in a designated meditation space, at a prescribed time of day.

Meditation carried out in an informal manner generally manifests as the practice of mindfulness. Mindfulness is the result of cultivating conscious awareness through the practice of formal meditation. When discussing mindfulness, our intent is to describe the state of being fully cognizant and actively involved in the present moment. The current moment represents the present time, the immediate NOW! The now constitutes the very existence of life. When one attains a state of mindfulness, it entails an elevated level of awareness towards the present moment and all corresponding occurrences within it.

For example, practicing mindfulness entails directing one's attention and maintaining a conscious awareness of the inhalation and exhalation process within the physical entity that houses the individual. It entails being conscious of the scent and flavor of food, of the hands in motion while cleaning the dishes, and attentively mindful of the physical actions of the body. Mindfulness can be attained through the act of actively engaging with the present moment.

When we propose engaging in the act of meditation, we are essentially conveying our intent to purposefully allocate a defined duration for the purpose of attentively acknowledging and comprehending an individual facet of existence. As previously noted, our state of consciousness in the present moment encompasses a wide range of possibilities. It could involve directing our attention to a physical or mental entity, focusing on the breath, contemplating a thought or emotion, visualizing something mentally or perceptually, or simply being cognizant of all occurrences in the present without singling out any particular phenomenon.

If you are inquiring about the benefits of being cognizant or deliberately observant of the present moment or a specific element of existence, the subsequent portion of this instructional document elucidates the manner in which meditation operates to enhance one's state of happiness, while also alleviating stress and anxiety.

The Scientific Study of Meditation

For an extensive duration spanning centuries, practitioners of meditation have consistently conveyed the myriad advantages derived from their meditative practice. For certain individuals, the practice of meditation can be perceived as a profoundly esoteric encounter, which renders it challenging to articulate. It has been reported that the benefits of these sessions are not limited to the duration of the sessions, but extend well beyond their conclusion. It has been purported that meditation expands one's perception beyond the bounds of the traditional five senses.

One can experience a profound sense of self-awareness, establish a deep connection with their inner being, and derive authentic happiness intrinsically, devoid of external dependencies. Given the peculiar and extraordinary nature of these advantages, scholars have endeavored to elucidate the scientific underpinnings of meditation. Their discoveries offer insight into the reasoning behind the capacity to experience healing, attain authentic happiness, or confront other intricate obstacles simply through the act of sitting.

Nevertheless, in spite of the varying identities and methodologies of these researchers, a consensus among all emerges affirming the existence and tangible benefits of meditation. As per the findings of these researchers, meditation holds the potential to induce alterations in the structural composition of the mind, bolster immune responses, enhance overall well-being, facilitate cognitive transformations, augment cortical volume, address depressive tendencies, alleviate stress, foster body-mind integration, and mitigate cognitive disruptions, all of which can be attributed to the phenomenon of neuroplasticity.

Modifications occurring within the cerebral structure

As per findings from neuroscientists, the practice of meditation serves to enhance the synaptic connections between the neuronal cells constituting the brain, thereby cultivating enhanced cognitive health and functionality. Subsequent research demonstrated that individuals who engage in consistent meditation practice exhibit enhanced levels of gyrification. Consequently, they exhibit enhanced cognitive processing capabilities, facilitating accelerated learning, superior recollection, and heightened comprehension. Based on numerous studies, meditation elicits positive neurophysiological alterations in the brain that yield advantageous outcomes for the individual.

Another study conducted in the year 2009 revealed a correlation between meditation and the growth of gray matter within the brain. Consequently, researchers propose that the heightened maturation of gray matter accounts for enhanced emotional, cognitive, and immune reactions. Given the crucial role of gray matter in central nervous system development, it can be inferred that it contributes to the cultivation of positive emotions, improved behavioral patterns, and enhanced emotional equilibrium.

In order to gain a more comprehensive understanding of how practitioners of meditation can attain these various advantages, researchers have taken additional measures to investigate the mechanisms by which meditation operates. It is noteworthy that meditation exerts influence beyond the neurochemical and physiological aspects of the brain. Neuroscientists have demonstrated that meditation induces changes in various brain functions as well. This signifies that meditation has the capacity to decelerate certain areas of the brain while simultaneously enhancing others. For instance, meditation is positively associated with reduced connectivity and network activity. These two functions pertain to disorders such as anxiety and actions encompassing the loss of focus.

Health Benefits

Several studies discussed earlier primarily concentrate on the neuro-cognitive dimension of meditation. Conversely, medical professionals and researchers have devoted their attention to exploring the health-related advantages of meditation. For instance, research has demonstrated that engaging in meditation enhances an individual's cognitive ability to retain information. In the year 2011, researchers examined individuals practicing focused attention meditation, specifically those who engaged in meditative practices. The individuals engaged in meditation practices for a duration exceeding five hours per day over the course of a three-month period. Following the conclusion of the designated time period, the participants underwent a series of assessments, which revealed a discernible enhancement in their ability to maintain voluntary attention.

An alternative study suggests that meditation operates similarly to a muscle, in that its strength and efficacy can be enhanced through increased frequency of practice. Fortunately, the duration of your meditation holds no significance, irrespective of whether it spans for 5 hours, 20 minutes, or even a mere 10 minutes. Research indicates that even a brief period of meditation, even as little as 10 minutes, can lead to noticeable improvements in stress reduction, enhancement of contemplative and mindfulness thinking, heightened sustained attention, enhanced memory, and relief from depression.

It does not come as a surprise, based on recent findings in meditation research, that individuals can effectively diminish stress levels even after participating in eight weeks of consistent meditation sessions. Based on the examination outcomes, individuals who engaged in meditation exhibited superior performance in demanding multitasking evaluations. Upon engaging in meditation, researchers have observed a decrease in the levels of cortisol, a stress hormone, providing a scientific rationale behind this phenomenon. By engaging in meditation prior to partaking in a demanding task, it is evident that there will be a discernible decrease in one's stress levels during the course of the activity.

Scientists elucidate that in order to attain optimal results from meditation, individuals ought to possess a thorough cognizance of their actions, objectives, and the manner in which meditation can facilitate the attainment of these advantages. Individuals who engage in meditation without a clear understanding of their desired outcomes are merely engaging in physical and mental exercises. A thorough comprehension of meditation can be attained by recognizing the pivotal function of the brain throughout the practice. While comprehending the impact of meditation on cognitive, physiological, and neurochemical processes, it becomes apparent that achieving stillness, maintaining silence, and cultivating introspective awareness are instrumental components.

Meditation - An All-Encompassing Phenomenon

Scientific inquiry has yielded findings that substantiate the advantageous impacts of meditation on both physiological and psychological well-being. Nonetheless, it should be noted that meditation also exerts a profound influence on an individual's disposition and overall life satisfaction. Through redirecting one's focus inward, the practice of meditation enables an enhanced understanding of the internal realm of thoughts and emotions, fostering a deeper sense of self-awareness. Through the enhancement of one's ability to focus, substantial levels of mastery and effectiveness can be attained across various domains of existence. Meditators assert a heightened sense of tranquility, inner harmony, equilibrium, and heightened mindfulness. They exhibit higher levels of eagerness and dynamism, along with a more robust understanding of their own capabilities. They experience a heightened sense of connectedness with the world.

All individuals who engage in the practice of meditation do so for assorted personal motivations. Numerous individuals engage in meditation due to its advantageous impact on holistic well-being and mental state. However, as one progresses in their meditation practice, these objectives may undergo transformations. Regardless of the underlying reasons, nonetheless, individuals who engage in regular practice of meditation will observe the comprehensive impacts.

Posture

The manner in which you engage in meditation should promote a tranquil, placid, yet attentive state of mind. This does not imply that one must assume the traditional lotus position, with each foot placed over the opposite thigh, a posture that can be quite uncomfortable for the typical Western individual who is not familiar with yoga. Although you may deem it worthwhile to exert oneself in acquiring proficiency in one of the prescribed postures involving crossed legs, no progress can be made by compelling one's body into an agonizing or unnatural position.

The optimal position for meditation entails maintaining a comfortable and motionless seated posture, with the spine erect, for approximately thirty minutes. With a resolute and motionless posture, the mind will naturally attain a state of unwavering composure. Maintaining an upright posture, characterized by a straight back without rigidity, while keeping the abdominal muscles relaxed, is regarded as highly crucial in the practice of meditation. This position will provide you with the opportunity to maintain a comfortable seated position over an extended duration, facilitating your ability to remain focused and alert. Additionally, it mitigates stress and fatigue by facilitating unobstructed circulation throughout the body. In certain systems, such as yoga, maintaining an upright posture of the spine is purported to yield spiritual advantages as well, as it enables enhanced facilitation of the "subtle" energy currents. Meditation may on occasion give rise to specific bodily adjustments. Commence by assuming the appropriate bodily alignment, however, should your head incline or waver during the course of meditation, it is advised not to oppose said movement, with the exception, naturally, of instances involving drowsiness or indolence.

All of the subsequent positions are appropriate for the practice of meditation. The utilization of a firm cushion or mat beneath the posterior region serves to enhance comfort and provide a sense of ease when assuming a seated position in any of the cross-legged postures. As the lotus posture and perfect posture are both considered traditional meditation positions, they are introduced initially. Nevertheless, the majority of individuals will likely find greater comfort in assuming a relaxed stance or utilizing a seated position on a chair. In the event that sitting is not conducive to your comfort, it is possible to recline on the floor in the shavasana ('corpse pose') position as an alternative for engaging in meditation. This role is highly straightforward and exceptionally calming, although the only drawback lies in its potential to induce somnolence.

Lotus posture (padmasana)

The stance of the lotus, as often portrayed with the Buddha, represents an optimal position for engaging in the practice of meditation. The legs are fused in unison, establishing a steadfast foundation that guarantees the meditator's unwavering stability, preventing any chances of toppling or succumbing to drowsiness, all without necessitating any exertion to sustain the posture.

After achieving a certain level of flexibility in the knees and ankles that permits easy maintenance of the posture, the pose becomes highly conducive to relaxation. Nevertheless, individuals who are solely accustomed to sitting on chairs may experience significant discomfort in the knee region initially, and it may take a substantial amount of time before they find the posture to be truly comfortable.

It is recommended to perform the preparatory exercises outlined, in order to loosen the joints of the hips, knees, and ankles, with the initial intention of assuming the lotus posture. Subsequently, it is suggested to gradually increase the duration of sitting in this posture, commencing with one minute and progressively extending it to two minutes, and beyond. It is strongly advised against forcefully placing your legs in this position, as it has the potential to result in severe harm.

Preparatory exercises

1. Assume a seated position on the floor, extending your legs in front of you. Flex the right knee and firmly hold the right ankle and foot with both hands. Position

the right ankle on the left leg, just above the knee, ensuring that the right foot gracefully extends beyond the leg. Maintain relaxation in the foot, ankle, and calf muscles as you grasp the right leg slightly above the ankle with your right hand, and proceed to rotate the right foot in alternating directions using your left hand. Perform ten repetitions in both directions, subsequently alternate legs and proceed with the exercise.

2. Assume a seated position on the ground, mirroring the stance demonstrated in Exercise 1. Proceed to flex the right knee, carefully positioning the ankle atop the left leg slightly above the knee joint. While maintaining a state of complete relaxation of the right leg, proceed to firmly grasp the right ankle using both hands, elevating it above the

leg and subsequently executing vigorous shakes to expel any looseness in the foot. Alternate legs and perform the exercise again.

3. Please assume a seated position on the floor, similar to the posture depicted in Exercise I, by bending your right knee and resting your right foot upon your left leg. While grasping the foot with the left hand and firmly encircling the leg with the right hand, securing the ankle, proceed to elevate the leg to its maximum height. Maintaining proper posture, articulate extensive circles with the foot, drawing it closer to the body at the highest point of the circle and further away at the lowest point. Perform the exercise ten repetitions on each leg consecutively.

4. Assume a seated position on the floor, extending your legs straight in front of you. Flex the right knee and position the right foot on the left thigh, in close proximity to the uppermost part of the leg. If required, provide support to your body by positioning the palms of your hands slightly behind and on the outer side of the buttocks. While maintaining an upright posture and ensuring that your right leg remains at ease, maintain this position for approximately one to two minutes, allowing the knee to descend towards the floor to the greatest extent possible. Alternate legs and perform the exercise again.

5. Assume the identical posture as in Exercise 4, albeit with the distinction that your body shall be upheld solely by the left hand, rather than both hands. Position the right hand on the right knee

and proceed to perform a series of gentle, rhythmic vertical movements, repeating this motion a total of ten times. Alternate the legs and perform the exercise once more.

6. Assume a seated position on the floor while extending your legs fully. Flex the knees outward and unite the soles of the feet. Without causing the soles to lose contact, bring them towards your body while aiming to position the heels as closely as feasible to the groin area. While grasping the toes with the hands, delicately oscillate the knees in an up and down motion, repetitively executing this action ten times with the objective of bringing the knees in close proximity to the floor.

7. Assume a seated position with your heels positioned adjacent to your groin, not dissimilar from Exercise 6. However, instead of grasping the toes, rest your hands upon your knees and exert slight pressure to further lower them towards the ground. Repeat ten times.

To assume the seated position with crossed legs, commonly known as the lotus posture

Assume a seated position on the floor, ensuring that your legs are fully extended in front of you. Flex the right knee and, while grasping the right foot with both hands, position it atop the left thigh in a manner where the heel exerts pressure on the abdomen. Next, in a comparable manner, position the left foot on the upper portion of the right thigh, ensuring that the heel firmly rests against the abdomen. It is important to elevate the soles of the feet and ensure that both knees make contact with the ground.

The posterior region ought to be maintained in a linear position, extending from the sacral area to the cervical vertebrae, while concurrently ensuring the abdominal muscles remain in a state of ease and relaxation. Ensure that the cranium aligns with the sacrum, maintaining a forward-facing gaze. The hands have the option to be positioned either upon the knees or betwixt the heels, with one hand atop the other.

Half lotus posture

Should you encounter any challenges while attempting to assume the full lotus posture, you might find it more suitable to initiate your practice with the half lotus position. Commence by performing the preliminary exercises outlined for the full lotus position in order to relax and prepare the body. Then sit on the floor with your legs stretched out in front of you. Flex the left knee and position the left foot beneath the right thigh in proximity to the buttocks to the maximum feasible extent. Subsequently, flex the right knee and position the right foot upon the left thigh, mirroring the posture of the complete lotus position. It is imperative that both knees are in contact with the ground while maintaining an upright posture, akin to the proper alignment observed in the full lotus position.

Perfect posture (siddhasana)

Assume a seated position on the floor, extending your legs straight in front of you. Flex the left knee, grasping the left foot with both hands, and position the heel against the perineum, which is located between the anus and the genitals. Subsequently, flex the right knee and position the heel in contact with the pubic bone. Position the toes snugly within the space formed by the calf and thigh of the left leg. Maintain an upright posture with a straight spine, and position the hands in the manner akin to that of the lotus position.

Easy posture

This is a straightforward sitting posture that involves sitting cross-legged with both feet resting on the ground. Similar to all meditation postures, it is important to maintain an upright yet supple posture, ensuring the back remains straight and avoiding any rigidity, while simultaneously allowing the stomach muscles to fully relax. The lower back muscles should bear the weight, while ensuring alignment of the head, neck, and trunk, creating a sense of the center of gravity passing from the base of the spine to the top of the head. One may opt to rest their hands either on their knees or in their lap, choosing between placing them one on top of the other or gently clasping them together.

Sitting on a chair

If it is not feasible for you toposition yourself on the floor, consider occupying a chair with a firm, upright backrest. Ideally, avail yourself of a specialized seating option like the posture chairs carefully crafted by Balans. These chairs devoid of backrests are equipped with slightly inclined seats and knee supports, effectively promoting an erect posture and maintaining an appropriate balance of body weight. Refrain from seating oneself in an armchair or on a plush sofa or bed. They will solely promote a hunched posture and lethargy, which is incongruous with the mental state sought after through meditation.

If you opt for a chair with an upright backrest, please ensure to assume a seated position towards the anterior section of the seat. The act of positioning a petite cushion at the rear of the chair, thus adopting a seated position closest to its front edge, can enhance your posture. Position your feet parallel to the ground, ensuring they are firmly planted with a slight distance between them, so that, in a relaxed state, your lower legs form a right angle with the floor. Maintain proper posture as demonstrated in the preceding stances.

Kneeling posture

Certain individuals perceive this particular stance as a viable substitute for the relaxed cross-legged posture, as it allows for a more effortless maintenance of proper spinal alignment. Assume a kneeling position with your knees firmly pressed together. Ensure that the heels are positioned apart, while aligning the big toes together in order to assume a seated position on the inner sides of the feet. Position the hands upon the knees whilst maintaining an upright posture akin to that described in the previous positions.

The Consequences of Receiving Divine Favor

The act of bestowing blessings leads us towards the subsequent objective:

- the embodiment of the celestial force within us. This fosters a profound and profound bond between us and the eternal realm, the omnipotent force, the hallowed essence, transcendent rapture, ethereal liberation, the realm of the Supreme Being, the enigmatic workings of the celestial realm, untainted and all-encompassing affection, as well as a profound spiritual perception of the presence of the divine.

- the pathway leading to a state of sanctity;

- the acceptance of the existence of miracles; • the conviction in the occurrence of miracles; • the faith in the possibility of miracles; • the trust in the occurrence of miracles; • the acknowledgment of the presence of miracles; • the assurance in the reality of miracles; • the confidence in the occurrence of miracles; • the understanding of the likelihood of miracles; • the persuasion in the existence of miracles.

- a comprehension of the profound enigmas underlying existence, the vital essence that permeates life, and the loftiest spiritual beliefs known as God-ism. ;

- the entrance to the realm of the state • the gateway to attaining a complete spiritual existence;

- celestial knowledge;

- inexplicable recoveries; • remarkable restoration of health; • extraordinary recuperations; • astonishing cures; • phenomenal regenerations.

- the stirring of the spirit;

- the manifestation of the Eternal Self, Atman – a divine essence bestowed by God the Father;

- the enhancement of the advantageous "psi" field; • the augmentation of the advantageous "psi" field.

- the enhancement of the advantageous "psi" field;

Procedures for the Implementation of the Craft of Bestowing Blessings

Here is an overview of the processes associated with the Blessing method:

- Our unwavering concentration is exclusively devoted to God the Father, as it is imperative to cultivate this internal disposition. • We diligently concentrate our attention on both the Anahata Chakra (located in the center of the chest) and the Sahasrara Chakra (situated at the crown of the head) simultaneously. Subsequently, following the recitation of the prescribed mantra, with closed eyes, we direct our visual attention towards Sahasrar, intentionally allowing our gaze to converge slightly. As the celestial energy begins to circulate throughout our being, our gaze naturally relaxes, while our eyes remain shut. Simultaneously, we experience an elevated state of consciousness, accompanied by a profound and varied sense of euphoria. Mentally repeating the Blessing formula with utmost sincerity, we raise our hand as directed. For individuals engaging in self-blessing, the energy becomes internalized within themselves.

• By diligently attending to the five stages of the manifestation of Divine Energy, we gain an acute awareness of the following: a. The progression leading to a climax; option b. reaching a climax; c. The observable decline; d. the conclusion of the manifestation; and e. the manifestation's global effects.

• In the event that the individual upon whom we bestow our blessings does not meet the criteria stated in the blessing formula, no visible manifestation or energetic exchange ensues. • Those individuals who do not engage in the practice of yoga are advised to direct their attention towards the regions encompassing the chest and the crown of the head, both internally and externally, in relation to their physical being. • Subsequent to the culmination of these five phases, the hand reverts to its customary position in a state of relaxation.

• In the final moments, we express our gratitude to God (it is not obligatory to recite the prayer of thanksgiving following every benediction, only at the conclusion).

The observed effects gradually intensify as time progresses. They possess a multitude of facets and exhibit diversity, thereby impacting not only the recipients but also the benefactors themselves for an extended duration spanning days, weeks, months, and even years. The extent of energy assimilation is limitless. The divine entity perpetually ensures an ample supply of energy for all individuals. Consequently, we have the liberty to conduct the Blessing at our discretion.

The Blessing encompasses more than mere supplication, for in our prayers lies the capacity to incur divine displeasure by inappropriately querying the Almighty. However, it is God who bestows upon us precisely what we require (by means of self-blessing) or grants those who are deemed blessed with what they need, all through the act of blessing. The assumption underlying the application of the Art of Blessing is that we possess the capacity for independent volition. There exists a popular adage in which individuals affirm that Divine benevolence can be bestowed upon us, yet it is not conveniently placed within our possession. Thus, the sole pathway to obtain something from the Divine is through the act of fervent supplication and entreaty.

In addition, residences, items, nourishment, circumstances, and deeds may also receive blessings, with an adaptation in the blessing formula employed in such instances. Due to the potential for divinization in any given scenario, the Energy of the Holy Spirit possesses the ability to be concentrated upon any object or situation. Due to the fact that the blessing pertains to the divine Spirit, who exists both within and beyond the realm of manifestation, and as it is an act performed directly by the divine, it is not imperative for a consecration to precede the bestowal of the blessing. By engaging in the practice of Blessing, we have the capability to awaken the latent energetic centers within us and establish a profound connection to the realm of synchronicity.

Suggested Role for Receiving a Benediction

• Endeavor to maintain a dignified and straight posture while standing with both feet planted firmly on the ground, one being the auspicious foot and the other being the one bringing blessings. Please strive to preserve a state of maximum relaxation while ensuring that your right arm is held in a lateral position, bent at a distance of 20 centimeters from the shoulder. Adopt a receptive hand posture, ensuring your fingers are gently flexed in a manner that allows for grasping. It is imperative that you adopt this stance from the outset of the conversation. If the avoidance of physical contact is desired or if the intention is to bestow blessings upon a limited group of individuals in close proximity, it is advisable to assume this recommended stance.

• In the event that the room accommodates a gathering exceeding fifty individuals or the recipient of the blessing happens to be a considerable distance away, it is advisable to stretch your arm forwards.

• During the execution of the Self-Blessing ritual, it is advised to maintain a posture in which your arms are kept alongside your torso, close to your body, in the same manner as you would typically hold them.

• Should you possess abundant vitality and possess adequate inner strength, it is expected that you shall have the ability to extend your right arm towards the individual you wish to bestow blessings upon. Aim to gently touch their forehead with your open fingers directed towards the Sahasrara, ensuring that you do not cover the crown of their head. It is recommended that you perform this action with your fingers directed towards Sahasrara.

It is imperative that you alleviate tension in your right arm and fingers to execute the exercise effectively.

Envision your distant loved one and strive to visualize their countenance, allowing you to impart your utmost well-wishes and blessings unto them. Envision the diverse individuals comprising the group if it is a gathering of individuals.

The proximity or distance between you and the other individual or group holds no inherent importance or meaning.

What Are The Advantages Of Utilizing Hypnosis?

The practice of hypnosis has evolved significantly over time, transitioning from a dubious stage trick into a resourceful tool with tangible benefits and practical applications in real-life contexts. The principal utilization of hypnosis is evident in the alleviation of discomfort and the management of pain, along with various other disorders specified herewith:

- In the management of chronic pain characterized by mild or severe symptoms
- Modifying behaviors related to the improper consumption of substances, including alcohol, etc.
- Assistance in fostering improved habits - Aid in developing healthier behaviors - Support in cultivating more positive routines - Guidance in establishing enhanced practices

"- In assisting with weight reduction - In aiding in weight loss - In facilitating the reduction of weight - In contributing to the lowering of body mass - In supporting individuals with weight management

- In striving to enhance one's overall way of life - In the pursuit of cultivating a more improved lifestyle - In the endeavor to create a superior quality of living

- In enhancing self-assurance and combating phobias and anxiety

- By enhancing self-confidence and confronting apprehension

- When it comes to the management of stress - Regarding the handling of stress - With regard to the effective management of stress - As for the proper management of stress - In the context of stress management - With respect to the effective handling of stress

- When dealing with psychological trauma - When confronting emotional distress - When addressing the effects of trauma - In the context of overcoming traumatic experiences - In the realm of battling psychological trauma - When attempting to overcome the challenges imposed by trauma - When engaging with the process of healing from trauma - In the pursuit of addressing and resolving trauma-related issues - In the sphere of combatting the negative impact of trauma

- In the treatment of depression
- When it comes to treating sleeping disorders and eating disorders
- When facing actual adversaries—sorrow and bereavement.

Hypnotic effects vary among individuals. Therefore, it is expected that the observed benefit may vary from individual to individual. The variations in the impact of hypnosis can be classified as follows...

In light of the Classic and Keto Diet, what distinguishes hypnosis as a superior alternative?

The utilization of hypnosis has been successfully extended to the realm of weight loss. In contrast to other methodologies, the utilization of hypnosis serves as a means to empower individuals in overcoming their challenges. The issue at hand is not your excess weight or obesity. The aforementioned are the indicative manifestations, whereas the root cause lies elsewhere. The issue stems from your lack of capacity to exert regulation over your dietary habits. Your inability to maintain an appropriate portion size while still experiencing satisfaction is the cause of your failure. It is within your discretion to have an additional indulgence. Your absence of drive to engage in physical exercise is evident. This refers to your circadian rhythm.

Through the utilization of hypnosis, one has the ability to focus extensively on each individual concern and effectively align oneself towards the intended outcome, namely achieving the desired weight. The ketogenic diet, which entails altering the body's food metabolic process, has the potential to produce outcomes; nonetheless, it is not universally recommended. Our physiological system metabolizes carbohydrates in order to produce energy. In the context of the ketogenic diet, we deprive our bodies of carbohydrates and replenish our energy reserves by consuming nourishing fats. In the absence of carbohydrates, our body seeks out the subsequent feasible alternative, which is fat. At this point, our physical system initiates the metabolic breakdown of fat as a means to generate energy. Numerous dieticians discourage the complete alteration of food processing. This necessitates a significant alteration in your dietary approach, wherein there is an escalation in the intake of fats and proteins, alongside a complete reduction in carbohydrates, a regimen that may not be suitable for all individuals.

Furthermore, considering an alternative candidate for a weight loss program such as:

- Low-calorie diet
- Diet that is low in fat or cholesterol
- Reduced sugar consumption - Diet with minimal sugar intake - Regimen with limited sugar content

- Diet low in carbohydrates
- A diet that restricts the intake of sodium significantly - A dietary regimen that emphasizes limited sodium consumption - A nutrition plan that advocates for reduced salt intake
- Diet rich in dietary fiber
- Diet rich in protein
- Diet specifically designed for individuals with diabetes - Specialized eating plan for those with diabetes - Prescribed nutritional regimen for managing diabetes

It has been noted that individuals belonging to varying age groups and genders exhibit distinct dietary preferences. Additionally, amidst numerous options, they may unwittingly combine several dietary plans, leading to heightened feelings of anxiety regarding their outcomes, ultimately resulting in premature abandonment.

The hypnosis-based weight loss program does not rely on you to make radical modifications. Over time, it intricately weaves its influence on your mind, molding your behavior and habits to conform to a well-suited way of life, ultimately leading to significant weight reduction. The results have been validated and are evident in the subsequent section.

Frequently Asked Questions Regarding Hypnosis

If I were to undergo hypnosis for weight loss, would I be at liberty to consume any food of my choosing without consequences

Response: The concept revolves around exercising restraint and exhibiting patience in regard to the approach. Hypnosis aids in the cultivation of a resolute and concentrated mindset, enabling one to prevail over temptations and make healthier choices in regard to eating habits, among other things. Hypnosis for weight loss will result in increased satisfaction and contentment with one's food consumption.

Does it involve surgery?

Response: Negative, in contrast to genuine lap band surgery or gastric band surgery, this entails a non-invasive approach as an alternative for achieving weight loss.

Is hypnotherapy a painful procedure?

Response: No, rather it induces a profound state of relaxation and a mild drowsiness.

Are there any potential adverse effects associated with the rapid weight loss program utilizing hypnosis?

Response: No adverse effects have been observed. Weight maintenance has been found to be improved through the utilization of hypnotherapy.

Is the employment of hypnosis in pursuit of weight loss considered to be a safe practice?

Response: Indeed, it is deemed to be secure.

Will I be subject to the hypnotherapist's influence?

Response: You consistently uphold your true nature and continually maintain composure and regulation.

Does the rapid weight loss system align with my suitability?

Response: The effectiveness of hypnosis varies among individuals, as it operates in unique ways based on their characteristics and responses. Certain individuals are prompt in embracing change, while others exhibit resilience and pose challenges in being assimilated into the group. However, the program is inclusive of all individuals.

What is the recommended duration of practice for achieving results in hypnosis?

Response: The exercise is contingent upon your vulnerability. The variation in this matter is subject to individual differences, rendering any universally applicable standard ineffective.

Is it guaranteed?

Response: It is highly unlikely for any practitioner to provide a guarantee of the outcomes. Based on the observed success rate, it is reasonable to infer that conducting the sessions meticulously should yield satisfactory outcomes.

When may I anticipate the occurrence of these changes?

Response: The outcomes will become apparent within a few weeks. Furthermore, without making any assumptions, it is important to acknowledge that the duration of hypnotherapy may vary in certain cases.

If I possess a pre-existing health condition, am I still able to choose this option?

Response: In general, the answer is affirmative. Nevertheless, it is advisable to seek guidance from the practitioner, providing them with comprehensive information, as the level of intensity may require modification according to your individual circumstances. It is employed even for conditions characterized by long-term or incurable pathological states, aiming to offer certain alleviation.

What is the optimal number of sessions required?

Response: A definitive response to this question is not readily available. The number of possible outcomes varies, contingent upon factors such as the objectives, your willingness to embrace the practice, and your susceptibility to hypnosis.

The Psychosocial Development Across The Lifespan

The Arc of Life

The Arc of Life is a curve that resembles the trajectory of a rainbow. The curvature of the neck, often referred to by medical professionals as the "arc of life," holds great significance as it signifies the point of origin for mental impulses emanating from the brain and traveling throughout the body. The absence of this curvature could potentially lead to adverse neurological consequences, impeding the transmission of neural signals along the spinal cord.

Additionally, it would be infeasible for you to properly maintain the equilibrium of your head's weight. Additionally, your intervertebral discs would be subjected to undue pressure throughout your entire body. These disks function as damping devices, enabling articulation and movement between your skeletal structures. Without delving any deeper, it becomes evident that the prominent, indispensable functions carried out by the arc of life positioned upon your neck are readily apparent.

Psychologists have embraced the idiomatic expression "arc of life" and employed it as a metaphor to denote significant concepts within the realm of psychology, as shall become evident.

From a psychological perspective, the Arc of Life denotes a trajectory delineated within life-span developmental psychology, placing particular emphasis on the processes of growth and transformation taking place over the entirety of one's lifespan. The human personality is perceived as the gradual development of potentiality throughout the course of life, spanning across a trajectory. The concept of the moment's cross-section is also employed to describe the nature of a distressing occurrence. This particular snapshot of the present moment may entail an occurrence such as the abrupt demise of a companion in a vehicular mishap, or it has the potential to encompass a prolonged period of time, such as the gradual deterioration of a friend diagnosed with cancer.

Irrespective of whether the occurrence is discrete or prolonged, each individual time segment encompasses the span of both historical, current, and future moments, thus resulting in what is referred to as temporal thickness. This implies that every noteworthy event in life transcends mere individual occurrences, as they have a historical and future continuum.

The concept of the life trajectory analogy can also be extended to situations where one makes a determination to undertake a particular task or address one or more needs. When you engage in this process, it is akin to tracing a path that extends from the present moment to the moment when you ultimately actualize and complete the implementation of that decision. If the choice is to embark on a leisurely stroll to a nearby park, the trajectory will be comparatively shorter and at a lower altitude in comparison to the path I would undertake when pursuing admission into graduate school to obtain a Ph.D. degree. During any given moment, the arcs that you sketch will possess activity at specific points along the trajectory. It is incumbent upon you to select either the arc or the location on which you will focus your attention.

According to this metaphor, your fundamental principles are exemplified by the longest arc you possess. The choice to embrace a fundamental principle is not to be taken lightly, as it entails committing to its adaptation and lifelong adherence. Hence, it can be deduced that the arc of greatest length directly signifies your intrinsic principles.

The arc also facilitates the cultivation of self-compassion and compassion towards others, particularly during instances when one may inadvertently stray from their core values. Consequently, it is not possible to have arcs that possess equal lengths. Shorter arcs facilitate incremental progress, allowing you to remain aligned with the overarching goals and objectives. Furthermore, it ensures the preservation of the fundamental principles.

The Psychological Study of the Lifespan

According to the theory of the Arc of life, individuals experience six distinct phases of personal psychological and spiritual development. This advancement assumes the shape of a curve. Individuals commence their existence equipped with an untainted sense of self, commonly referred to as the "pristine ego," which encompasses their inherent spiritual, transcendent, or authentic nature. Concurrently, this innate disposition is accompanied by a notable level of spiritual consciousness. In due course, a spurious persona arises, and under its sway, an individual manifests preoccupation with material possessions and mundane circumstances. In the final phase, individuals who persist in their growth undergo a process of readjustment and reintegration with the original realm of the spiritual dimension.

A significant number of individuals are unable to transcend the realm of mundane aspirations and ultimately yield to the norms and customs prevalent within their respective societies. Some individuals may even relinquish their previously cherished sense of affiliation in order to attain a certain level of autonomy and exercise their own judgment. A small faction, potentially increasing in numbers, takes it a step further and endeavors to reintegrate, with the aspiration of attaining a harmonious synthesis with the natural world, upon their spiritual return.

Attaining any significant landmark along this course of progression frequently necessitates individuals to release their dislikes and attachments, resulting in a somewhat arduous experience. This decline is frequently enforced by distressing circumstances such as physical injury, illness, adversity in various forms, and the approach of mortality. This voyage is notably challenging, yet there are scarce instances, if any, in which individuals express remorse for embarking upon this expedition. Nevertheless, one advantageous aspect of this approach is its ability to elicit an individual's most genuine essence and sincere principles.

Allow me to present to you the order of priorities regarding the pursuit of the "meaning of life" as one traverses through the chapters of existence.

Primary concerns in infancy: The stage of infancy is characterized by egocentrism, wherein the primary focus lies on aspects related to survival, safety, comfort, and the differentiation between spiritual and daily consciousness. During the early stages of human development, individuals are primarily preoccupied with the pursuit of solace, security, and the fulfillment of their basic needs for survival. Additionally, they strive to discern between mundane aspects of life and the realm of spiritual consciousness, and to gratify their innate preferences and aversions.

During childhood, the main focus lies in acquiring knowledge about various aspects of the world, encompassing its general features as well as specific elements, including rules, traditions, and conventions. As focus wanes and evolves into heightened spiritual consciousness, the passage of time leads to the gradual fading of scientific, secular, and materialistic inclinations and perspectives. This subsequent phase is referred to as the conditioning phase.

Precedence during the stage of conformity and early adulthood. This phase entails cultivating and reinforcing preexisting aversions and attachments that align with a natural inclination toward enhancing our social integration and personal satisfaction. These aspirations are fulfilled through the acquisition of material wealth and social status, the attainment of esteemed alliances, and the refusal or disavowal of what might seem incongruous or unfamiliar.

The phase of late adulthood, commonly referred to as the individual stage, encompasses the process of self-development and self-discovery as one assumes the role of a conscientious and autonomous observer and participant in one's own life. By engaging in this action, you are voluntarily surrendering your previous connections and adapting to the associated uncertainty and relatively solitary environment.

The initial stage of maturity, known as the integration phase, entails a comprehensive reassessment of one's conduct and principles through a universal lens, resulting in a gradual synchronization of one's lifestyle with the most elevated altruistic principles.

During the phase of universal or complete maturity, there is a focus on prioritizing universal significance and quality. During this stage, one comprehends and fully embraces the profound significance of life. An individual begins to place a higher value on existence rather than attainment or action, and embracing the present transcends the apprehension of loss and mortality. In addition, individuals begin to exemplify empathy, and as a result, they organically assume the role of wise mentors. They additionally provide assistance to individuals in conquering spiritual unease and mending psychological injuries.

These individuals emerge as valuable assets to both their immediate and distant communities due to the significant impact they wield through their literary works and oratory skills. An individual in this collective realm possesses the capacity to demonstrate empathy and actively participate in the burdens of others, even while attaining a state of inner tranquility, happiness, and embracing realities. He refrains from pursuing additional rewards and strives to create a comfortable environment for those in his presence.

Meditation And Success

In a tranquil room situated within the confines of Silicon Valley, computer programmers congregate, adopting a serene posture with legs gracefully crossed and eyes entranced, enveloped by a profound silence. They are attentively perceiving the auditory sensation originating from their own respiration. In an alternative scenario, a proprietor of a regional real estate establishment initiates her day by engaging in focused respiration exercises and performing a series of yoga postures.

Meanwhile, in another location, a diligent individual employed as a data entry specialist concludes the consumption of his turkey sandwich. Subsequently, he returns to his designated workstation, dons his headphones, and deliberately inhales, finding solace in the serene auditory experience of cascading water and resonating bells.

Every individual holds a unique perception regarding the visual representation of meditation, yet it is undeniable that its widespread acceptance within Western society is growing swiftly. Enhanced productivity, reduced levels of stress and sadness, and alleviation of physical discomfort such as headaches and muscular tension are among the numerous benefits it offers in both professional and personal realms.

When the term "meditation" is mentioned, it often conjures images of devout individuals engaged in a tranquil state within distant, celestial sanctuaries. It may exude an air of exoticism and seem unattainable within the context of everyday existence, rendering it challenging to comprehend its potential for personal or professional advancement. One's cultural or spiritual beliefs, as well as prior conceptions regarding the nature of meditation, may lead to reluctance in participating in this practice. Despite the foundational principles of meditation being derived from diverse spiritual traditions, scientific research is revealing the multitude of health benefits associated with regular engagement in this practice of focused and relaxed contemplation. Consequently, healthcare professionals in Western medicine are progressively endorsing its usage.

Regardless of whether your intention is to engage in meditation for spiritual enlightenment or to attain physical and mental well-being, the practice commonly encompasses the following elements:

Tranquil Environment: Whether amidst nature, adjacent to a body of water, within a serene studio, or in the comfort of your own living space, meditation is commonly undertaken in an environment that offers physical comfort and tranquility. Certain individuals opt to engage in quiet seated meditation on a cushion, directing their focus towards their breath, while others may select the alternative of reclining in bed and indulging in the harmonizing melodies of calming music.

Body position and motion: Typically, during a mediation session, a participant assumes a specific posture, characterized by crossed legs, an upright spinal alignment, and placing their hands calmly on their knees. On certain occasions, participants may assume a reclined position or engage in specific bodily movements reminiscent of those found in yoga or t'ai chi.

In the context of meditation, the individual will direct their awareness towards various elements, including their breath, the perceptible flow of energy within their physical being, an external object, a guiding principle or abstract concept, or a designated word or phrase referred to as a mantra.

An unbiased mindset: In the practice of meditation, the individual's mind remains receptive to thoughts, allowing them to arise and dissipate without engaging in any form of critical evaluation. Rather than suppressing the thoughts, the meditator will often opt to acknowledge them and subsequently redirect their focus towards the initial objective.

How Meditation Increases Success

Terms such as "tenacity," "diligence," "exertion," and "objective-oriented behavior" are commonly linked to the concept of prevailing, accomplishing one's intentions, or attaining the desired mindset. It is highly conceivable that meditation would not be among the top 100 words correlated with success. However, it is imperative that it should be.

Consider this. Wouldn't it be reasonable to consider that the potential effects of engaging in a singular exercise that concurrently improves various facets of your mental and physical well-being, encompassing areas such as blood pressure, immunity, headaches, problem-solving aptitude, and overall creativity, could have a substantial influence on your overall performance in life? The higher the level of your physical well-being and personal empowerment, the greater the likelihood of successfully attaining your self-determined objectives.

Optimizing the Benefits of Meditation

Despite its potential to be a time-consuming pursuit, meditation need not monopolize extensive portions of your daily schedule. Engaging in a brief meditation session, lasting approximately ten to fifteen minutes, can yield noticeable relaxation benefits.

We present a compendium of various meditation methods herein, serving as a comprehensive instructional resource for your reference. Please consider including one or two options that you find appealing in your calendar. To commence the day with a constructive outlook, numerous individuals prefer engaging in meditation as their first act upon awakening. Some individuals opt to engage in meditation prior to sleep in order to alleviate mental restlessness and achieve a tranquil state conducive to peaceful slumber. Subsequently in Chapter 3, several meditation techniques are delineated.

The Practice of Meditation

Engaging in deep breathing or breath focus entails the act of closing your eyes and directing your complete concentration towards the experience of your breath as it flows into and out of your lungs. The vast majority of meditation techniques are founded upon this principle, and numerous others further elaborate upon it.

Body Scanning: Primarily employed for relaxation purposes. It involves directing one's attention towards multiple body regions sequentially, inducing a deliberate contraction followed by release for each, while attentively observing the accompanying sensations.

Energy Concentration: Directing one's attention towards the flow of energy within oneself and experiencing a sense of being "attuned" or "rooted," denoting a state of composure and assurance. Furthermore, it could involve the utilization of Hindu traditions, wherein the concept of 'chakras' or energy centers is applied.

Observing: This variation of the Breath Focus technique entails maintaining a steady gaze. Individuals have the option to either maintain an open-eyed stance or direct their gaze towards a particular object.

Mental imagery: This encompasses the process of shutting your eyes and directing your focus towards a mental portrayal of a serene location, such as a beach, a mountain, or a cherished hiking trail.

Guided Imagery, also referred to as supervised visualization, entails the utilization of an instructor or a prerecorded session to guide individuals through tranquil mental imagery and engage their sensory faculties.

Chanting: This pertains to the practice of continuously and rhythmically uttering a word, syllable, or phrase either mentally or verbally.

Music: This entails directing your focus towards controlled breath regulation while experiencing serene auditory compositions such as chiming bells, enchanting harps, melodious stringed instruments, soothing wind instruments, and blissful natural sounds.

Yoga embodies a form of meditation, as deliberate and methodical movements are executed in tandem with the breath and mindful awareness of the body's energy. It is most effective when paired with soothing music or a breathtaking natural environment.

T'ai Chi, an ancient discipline blending meditation and martial arts, facilitates the practitioner's focus on harnessing the intrinsic energy flowing within the body.

Qi Gong is an integrative practice that incorporates controlled breathing, fluid bodily movements, focused meditation, and effective relaxation techniques, all working in harmony to restore and sustain equilibrium. Centrally situated along the spinal column, torso, and forehead, the core of Chinese cultural beliefs revolves around the concept of Qi—revered as an embodiment of energy.

Walking Meditation: By directing one's attention solely to the physical sensations of movement and allowing all other thoughts to naturally dissipate, walking can be employed as a form of meditative practice. This exercise is highly versatile as it can be performed while walking along the corridors at work, on the pavement, or in the natural environment.

Insight or Mindfulness Meditation involves cultivating a heightened state of awareness towards the unpredictable movement of one's own thoughts, emotions, and experiences. It places emphasis on the present moment, distinct from preceding or forthcoming occurrences.

Positive affirmations involve focusing on constructive thoughts that will aid in the achievement of your goals. I have achieved considerable success, garnered admiration, and possess the ability to accomplish this task as well as any other challenge I choose to undertake.

Engaging in Contemplative Study: involves perusing poetry, religious literature, or excerpts from sacred texts, and carefully examining their profound meaning or personal impact. This may be complemented by attending poetry readings, listening to devotional music, or engaging in written expression.

Embodied Tranquility: This methodology involves cultivating a state of equilibrium and inner grounding, followed by allowing your physique to gracefully engage in multi-directional movements, all whilst focusing on the intricate sensations coursing through your corporeal vessel.

Meditation

The film revolves around a female protagonist, portrayed by the esteemed actress Julia Roberts, who experiences a divorce and seeks to embark on a journey of self-discovery and self-renewal. Therefore, she intends to embark on a three-month excursion, devoting one month each to Italy, India, and Bali. Her notion entailed that she would allocate her time in Italy for the purpose of rediscovering her fervor for gastronomy. She intended to dedicate her time in India to immersing herself in the teachings of the Buddha at a monastery, concluding her journey in Bali where she would reunite with a revered, acquainted monk of great wisdom. This proposition appears to be an excellent concept, and indeed, ever since the film's premiere, it has emerged as a prevailing trend for holiday arrangements.

Approximately midway through the film, Julia Roberts finds herself at the monastery in India and endeavors, albeit with limited success, to engage in the practice of meditation. She assumes a seated position within the meditation room, proceeds to shut her eyes, and encounters the inevitable challenge of quieting her thoughts. Her thought process transitions swiftly from contemplating the creation of a dedicated space for meditation to surreptitiously observing others and pondering the reasons behind their successful meditation practices, which elude her. Experiencing a sense of vexation, she rises abruptly and departs from the meditation room in a gust of emotion.

What is the reason for me divulging this information to you? Initially, it is crucial to comprehend and acknowledge that the sensations experienced by Julia Roberts during her initial attempt at meditation will equally be experienced by oneself. You may experience a sense of ennui or exasperation. Your thoughts will persistently occupy your mind, as you anticipate an elusive moment of clarity that will not materialize. You shall find frustration directed towards those who effortlessly demonstrate mastery and question the plausibility of achieving a state of mind devoid of thoughts. Such is the nature of the initial experiences in the practice of meditation.

Meditation is akin to a muscle that requires development through training. The greater the amount of training dedicated to that muscle, the more robust and resilient it will grow. For instance, upon entering the gym for the first time, it would not be advisable to emulate Arnold Schwarzenegger's rigorous training regimen during his bodybuilding competitions. It is highly likely that you will sustain significant injuries and have to exert considerable effort to return to your place of residence. It is advisable to commence your workout routine by utilizing the lightest weights available at the gym. Once you have developed a sense of comfort and have become acquainted with this initial weight, you can gradually progress by incrementing the weight by one kilogram at a time.

The aforementioned statement applies equally to the practice of meditation. We do not advise planning to meditate for half an hour during your first session as it is highly probable that you will relinquish after a mere two minutes. Embarking on the journey of practicing meditation can be initiated from its very inception, and one should not harbor any sense of shame in doing so. Indeed, there is no disgrace in encountering any of the exasperating emotions that accompany one's initial foray into meditation. The first rule pertaining to meditation can be stated as follows:

Exhibit patience and refrain from passing judgment upon oneself.

It is entirely commonplace for the mind to stray during the practice of meditation. We do not possess the ability to govern our thoughts. Therefore, when a thought arises during the practice of meditation, it is important to recognize and acknowledge the thought, together with the slight diversion of the mind, and subsequently redirect your attention back to the meditation.

How Do I Meditate?

Now that you have been acquainted with the forthcoming aspects of your initial meditation session, let us delve into the specific activities you will be engaging in. There exist a wide array of meditation variations, with varying degrees of spirituality. The two prevailing forms of meditation are "Transcendental Meditation" and "Mindfulness Meditation." In the context of this book, we shall primarily focus on the latter i.e., "Mindfulness Meditation."

Mindfulness meditation involves the cultivation of mindfulness, extending beyond the actual moments of meditation. The objective is for you to integrate mindfulness into your daily routine. The most straightforward approach to commence the practice of mindfulness involves engaging in meditation, gradually integrating it into your daily routine over time.

For the initial session of meditation, it is advisable to assign a duration of five minutes by utilizing a timer. Moreover, there are excellent meditation applications available for download on your mobile device, which feature integrated timers. I hold great admiration for Sam Harris' "Waking Up" app for meditation, which I consider to be one of my preferred choices (Waking up, 2020). It is equipped with a beginner's program tailored specifically for individuals who are new to the practice of meditation, such as yourself. Prior to proceeding with app downloads or enrolling in courses, it is imperative that you gain a clear comprehension of the meditation process and the activities involved.

Prior to commencing your meditation session, it is imperative to secure a suitable, relaxed posture. Engaging in a supine position for meditation, particularly for those who are inexperienced, carries the potential of succumbing to drowsiness. Feel free to adopt any seated position that is most comfortable for you, be it on a chair, leaning against a wall, or even on the floor if you prefer. Provided that one is capable of maintaining an upright posture and attaining a state of comfort, meditation is viable. The predominant posture adopted during meditation often entails sitting on the ground, cross-legged, while allowing the hands to rest serenely either on the lap or thighs.

The location in which you choose to engage in meditation bears little significance. Once you have acquired the proficiency in the practice of meditation, you will find yourself capable of engaging in it regardless of your current location. Indeed, even within the confines of a construction site. Nevertheless, as a novice, it would be advisable to locate a location that is moderately tranquil and devoid of excessive commotion. Feel free to indulge in serene classical melodies or calming natural sounds as you embark on your meditation session. Nevertheless, it is advisable to refrain from selecting music that may prove excessively diverting, such as songs with lyrics or excessively vigorous rhythms. Subsequently, you initiate the practice by focusing on one's breath.

In your estimation, how frequently do you observe your respiration during the course of a day? Once a day? Maybe twice? There is no adverse consequence in stating that you are completely unaware of it—let us recall the primary principle of refraining from making any judgments.

The breath is important. In addition to the vital aspect of sustaining our existence, naturally. It holds significance within the practice of meditation, for it serves as a steadfast reference point that facilitates the recovery of concentration in instances of mental distraction. Therefore, the initial step upon assuming a posture for meditation is to direct your focus towards your breath. Do not excessively concern yourself with the manner in which you are inhaling and exhaling initially. Commence by merely experiencing the inhalation and exhalation of the breath. Where do you experience the highest concentration of your respiration? Can you perceive it on the surface of your nose or deep within your throat? Perchance you perceive the most notable presence of your breath within your chest. There are no incorrect responses in this context. Simply just feel.

After acquiring knowledge of the sensory perception of the breath, you may proceed by directing your focus towards the rhythm of your respiration. Are your respiratory cycles characterized by brevity and superficiality? Alternatively, do they consist of prolonged, profound inhalations that resound within the depths of your abdomen? Whilst it is a commonly held notion that breathing is merely an act of inhalation and exhalation, it is essential to observe that there exists an additional aspect of breathing that often goes unnoticed.

There exists a temporary cessation of airflow between the act of exhaling and the subsequent inhalation. Therefore, during a brief interval, respiration will cease entirely. Therefore, the pattern consists of alternating inhalation, exhalation, and momentary cessation, as opposed to solely inhalation and exhalation. These subtleties will become apparent to you as you engage in mindful observation during your meditation practice.

During the initial five-minute meditation session, the following activities are recommended. Merely adhere to the rhythm of your respiration. If one becomes immersed in contemplation, it is completely acceptable. It is integral to the iterative journey of acquiring meditation skills. Take cognizance of the idea that has occurred to you and recognize that you have veered off track. Subsequently, redirect your focus towards attending to your breath.

Whilst engaged in meditation, one must not solely focus on respiration, but commencing with the breath proves most advantageous as it offers a rhythmic, trackable stimulus. As you continue to engage in your meditation practice, you will be requested to direct your attention towards the auditory stimuli in your surroundings. Furthermore, it is expected that you direct your focus towards your visual surroundings, including situations where your eyes are shut.

Even when engaged in a state of quietude, there are auditory stimuli you shall perceive. It is possible that you may perceive the auditory presence of your respiration and the pulsations of your cardiovascular system. There is a possibility that you may experience a subtle buzzing or ringing originating from your ears. In due course, you will become aware of the auditory presence of vehicles traversing, airplanes passing overhead, and the gentle rustling of the wind amid the foliage. These are all sounds of which we might not have been cognizant if it had not been for the discipline of mindfulness.

Similar observations can be made when requested to direct your attention toward your visual domain while your eyes are in a closed state. Even in a state of occlusion, visual perception persist, as complete darkness does not prevail. If you are able to do so, you will recognize the presence of darkness and gain insight regarding its vast extent. Should you choose to recline outdoors during daylight hours, and gently close your eyes, it is possible that your vision will unveil hues of orange, tinged with faint traces of green. It is not solely concerned with perception, but rather the nature of what is perceived and the manner in which one experiences their visual domain.

Following Your Breath

I distinctly remember experiencing a sense of being overcome as a young child when I became acutely aware of my own respiration. This was the inaugural instance in which I truly acknowledged its presence. Initially, I was filled with fear as I attempted to divert my attention to alternative thoughts, employing the technique I employ when seeking to abate hiccups. However, to my astonishment, I became entranced with the serene ebb and flow of my respiration, which seemed to occur effortlessly, independent of any deliberate effort on my part. It was hypnotizing. Additionally, I found it somewhat disconcerting, primarily due to the fact that this heightened level of consciousness presented a distinct sensation that starkly contrasted with my usual, mundane experience of being engrossed in my own thoughts. Indeed, it is true that my focus quickly diverged towards whimsical fancies; however, upon reflecting upon this occurrence, I have come to recognize it as one of my initial instances of mindful consciousness. As a young individual, the magnitude of this experience was overwhelming. However, embracing the practice of observing my breath has evolved into a source of stability and enlightenment, facilitating my capacity to navigate each moment with deliberate intention.

*

Cultivating a conscious mindfulness of your breath constitutes a fundamental approach to engage in meditation, coupled with the practice of observing thoughts without attachment, akin to our previous discussion on vehicles traversing the road. Therefore, it is logical to conclude that incorporating focused attention on your breath presents itself as a convenient method to cultivate a mindful state throughout your day, even outside designated meditation sessions. To elaborate, practicing mindfulness.

This marks the initial among eleven techniques that we will examine, all of which can be implemented at any point throughout your day, in order to cultivate a habitual state of mindfulness.

As you may envision, the practice of being mindful of your breath is one that can be carried out in any location without constraint. Lying in bed. Sitting at your desk. Navigating through the corridor in your professional setting. Lounging on your couch. Surrounded by familiar faces in the comfort of one's own residence or amidst the hustle and bustle of a vibrant dining establishment.

On a plane. On a hike. On a happy day. On a terrible day. Literally anywhere, anytime.

Frequently, we consciously interrupt our activities to pause momentarily and catch our breath. This typically occurs in moments of intense stress as a means to reground ourselves and alleviate the accelerated pace of our heartbeat. Prior to a significant presentation, prior to proceeding down the aisle. Possibly subsequent to a difficult dialogue or in preparation for initiating one.

Why procrastinate until we are all agitated? This reminds me of my earnest yet ineffective and fruitless endeavors to relax during the period of enduring a migraine. In my endeavors to alleviate discomfort, I endeavor to gently manipulate the muscles in my neck or apply lavender oil, with the intent of inducing a state of relaxation. These efforts are typically employed when I find myself in a state of physical distress, compelling me to recline in bed in a posture resembling that of a fetus. I am gradually improving in adopting a more intelligent approach, which involves incorporating regular relaxation and pain reduction techniques into my daily routine, even during periods of peak well-being. By doing so, I endeavor to minimize the severity of subsequent migraines or potentially prevent their occurrence altogether.

*

Simply being conscious of the act of breathing is all that is necessary. Simple and relaxing. Perceiving it during your inhalation and exhalation. Investigating the extent to which one can vividly perceive and immerse oneself in an experience, and discerning the multitude of intricate details that can be perceived.

I have a strong inclination towards ensuring thoroughness in this context. While meditation involves allowing it to occur, in the practice of mindfulness, we strive to examine and approach our breath with a sense of curiosity.

Initiate the observation of your breath as you engage in the act of reading at this present moment.

As soon as the sensation of coolness greets your nostrils upon inhaling. The sensation of the air moving through the pharyngeal region. The minute force exerted in your throat as it descends. The initial indication of an elevation in the chest and abdomen as the lungs are filled with air. The soft expansion. Providing your entire body with ample amounts of fresh oxygen. The sensation of complete lung expansion. The period of reflection prior to the act of expiration. Subsequently, the initiation of the expiration process itself. The descent of your abdomen and thorax, induced by the upward displacement of the diaphragm, facilitates the exhalation of the recently warmed air, directed back up the pharynx and expelled through the nasal cavity once more.

Seek to establish a position with one hand resting upon your abdomen and the other hand positioned upon your chest. During inhalation, endeavor to direct your attention towards the expansion and nourishment of your abdomen. We have a tendency to engage in shallow breathing, primarily focusing on our chest rather than taking complete, profound breaths, especially during periods of anxiety or when our minds are preoccupied. When I experience anxiety, I frequently notice that I restrict my breathing to a shallow depth, focusing solely on utilizing the uppermost portion of my lungs. In response, my shoulder muscles become tense in order to make up for it. Placing a hand on the abdomen can facilitate the cultivation of a practice wherein one learns to engage in deeper respiratory patterns. During moments of unease or distress, employing a gentle touch on the abdomen can alleviate troubling feelings in conjunction with controlled breathing. Incorporating a more measured and profound inhalation helps to pacify the body promptly, effectively disengaging it from the state of heightened arousal commonly known as fight or flight response. It merely requires a matter of seconds.

At any moment that you recollect, be it while engaged in household chores, running errands, or attending a professional meeting, inhale deeply, allowing the breath to expand within your abdomen. Nice and slow. It will promptly redirect your attention to the current moment, and through consistent reinforcement, you will increasingly develop a propensity to experience these fleeting instances of self-awareness throughout your daily routine. These instances accumulate over time and will swiftly furnish you with a means to recalibrate and unwind your mind within a mere fraction of a moment's cognizance.

The Various Strata Of Our Being

As stated in the introductory chapter, our existence extends beyond the individual realm and transcends mere micro entities. Rather, we inhabit a macrocosmic sphere where we are intricately intertwined with all facets of the cosmos. We engage in a continuous exchange of information, albeit on a subconscious level. We are engaged in the dissemination of knowledge with the trees, plants, animals, other entities, the natural realm, and various objects. And these genetic imprints are stored within our DNA. Likewise, the genetic heritage of our forebears, as well as the imprints carried within our DNA, exemplify this notion. We also bear those imprints within ourselves. These impressions exert a considerable influence on our lives, regardless of our conscious recognition of it. For instance, during the act of embracing a tree, a significant amount of information is mutually conveyed. Vigorously, it is imparting the knowledge it has acquired to us. We may lack the ability to articulate such information, however, we experience a sense of comfort and belonging.

One additional illustration arises when we embark on an excursion to a site of historical significance, as it facilitates the transference of historical events and the accompanying sentiments experienced by individuals during that era. All of this interaction takes place at a more profound level. And it demonstrates our interconnectedness with both the micro and macro aspects of existence.

When one finds oneself in a location where one's forebears resided, a multitude of sentiments surge forth, leading to a profound sense of being emotionally inundated. The rational faculty is unable to promptly assimilate this information, emotions, and sentiments. Subsequently, one comprehends, and rationally perceives sensations of affection, sorrow, or an inherent sense of absence. This substantiates the coexistence of our being across various planes simultaneously. "We can succinctly outline our various states of being as follows:

1) Individual Current Existence: This stratum is in immediate proximity, and we can intimately experience its presence. We possess awareness of our physical, mental, and emotional state, as we have the capacity to observe, perceive, and utilize all five of our sensory faculties. The current situations and circumstances that are unfolding are collectively encompassing our present state. The present life we have is composed of our experiences from childhood, adolescence, and adulthood. While one may lack conscious recollection of specific aspects of their early childhood, this period still contributes to their current personal existence. The emotions and feelings we have encountered are all inherently stored within our physical entities. Every single moment of this existence, starting from the moment of our conception, constitutes an integral

component of our current personal existence. Although we may not consciously recollect the emotions and feelings, it does not negate our prior encounter with them.

Our cellular memories retain our complete range of accomplishments, adversities, afflictions, sentiments of devotion and concern, amongst other experiences. For instance, in your earliest stages of life, it is probable that you accompanied your parents to a particular location. The ordeal proved to be distressing due to the unforeseen inclement weather, causing you to become exceedingly sick. It is likely that upon revisiting this location in adulthood, one may initially experience a sense of heaviness without fully comprehending the reasons behind it. This phenomenon can be attributed to the reenactment of deep-seated emotions and feelings entrenched within your cellular memories.

2) Previous incarnations: As souls, we do not solely experience our current

existence, but have undergone numerous previous lives in varying physical forms, diverse cultural environments, and amidst an array of historical periods and geographical locations. In order to experience growth and maturation on a spiritual level, we have undergone multiple incarnations, where each existence is dedicated to the pursuit of predetermined objectives and the acquisition of profound insights. All of these recollections are ingrained within our subconscious cognition, which can be attained by means of profound contemplation or via various therapeutic modalities, such as Past Life Regression. The knowledge and expertise acquired from our previous existences have also become deeply ingrained within our beings. Indeed, there are occasions when we tangibly sense the existence of those recollections. We also possess the inclination to perpetuate the recollections, perceptions, and consequences of our previous incarnations. They are excessively ingrained in our cellular memories. There are instances in which we engage in actions driven by the influences of our previous incarnations.

For instance, when embarking on a journey to a new location, there is an inexplicable sense of familiarity, as if one has resided here before. You possess knowledge of several notable landmarks and are able to seamlessly integrate into the local community without delay. Although there may not be a conscious connection to that location, the activation of your past life memory occurs. Perhaps there exists a previous existence in which you have resided within that location, thus accounting for its comforting ambiance. An additional illustration would pertain to a fear that lacks any association with one's current circumstances, such as the fear of heights, fear of water, or any other phobia.

Naturally, the apprehensions, aversions, or psychological scars that you carry can be effectively addressed through therapeutic intervention, thereby obviating the necessity of delving deeper into them.

3) Genetic Code: The comprehensive collection of imprints, experiential memories, emotional states, sensations stored within our genetic code, inherited from our progenitors, forefathers, predecessors, and all individuals linked by our genetic heritage, fundamentally shapes our state of being. These imprints play a significant role in determining aspects of our personality, such as our appearance, temperament, and even cognitive patterns. Irrespective of personal preferences, our inherent allegiance is instinctively directed towards our genetic ancestry. Indeed, as spiritual beings, we deliberately determine our genetic makeup and select our guardians in order to fulfill our objectives in accordance with our prior existence encounters and the wisdom we must acquire for continued growth.

For instance, consider that in this present existence our principal objective is to develop the ability to relinquish detrimental relationships while maintaining self-compassion. Subsequently, we will select a familial structure wherein we can discern the presence of detrimental elements stemming from our parents who continually assume the role of our critics. The underlying message is to refrain from absorbing unfounded criticism and negative emotions emanating from such individuals. Nevertheless, we should express appreciation for the gift of life bestowed upon us by others and demonstrate kindness and understanding towards ourselves.

One instance that can be employed to comprehend the impact of epigenetics or DNA on our being is our extensive array of preferences and aversions. Your paternal grandfather had a deep affection for strawberries, a sentiment that was similarly shared by your father. Now, it seems that you are the next in line within our lineage to develop an ardent fondness for this fruit. In a similar vein, your grandmother on your mother's side harbored an aversion towards even the most minute traces of dust within the household. Your mother adhered to an identical sequence, and now you are poised to follow suit. These illustrations were merely elemental in nature; however, it should be noted that even traumatic experiences are imprinted within an individual's genetic material. The emotional residue of natural disasters or conflicts would persist within our beings if any members of our family were impacted by such cataclysmic events.

A further instance of the intergenerational transmission of trauma is exemplified by a familial unit that witnessed the ravages of war within their local community. The majority of the family members perished, prompting the surviving members to seek refuge in secure locations in order to ensure their own survival. In this instance, should such a circumstance arise, the intergenerational transmission of trauma may manifest itself in future generations. This transmission could result in an unwarranted sense of insecurity regarding their livelihood and survival, or a constant feeling of incompleteness in the place they now call home. Despite the lack of awareness among future generations regarding the past, it is worth noting that these very sentiments and emotions continue to reside within them. Undoubtedly, each of us will possess one or more instances within this particular framework.

Allow me to offer an additional noteworthy illustration pertaining to the apprehension individuals may hold in relation to success or failure. There is consistently a heightened likelihood of individuals from previous generations encountering significant setbacks following a period of notable achievements, or alternatively, failing to achieve any form of success despite exerting considerable effort. In either scenario, the ensuing emotional distress resulting from experiencing failure or the loss of success will be imprinted within the individual's genetic material. An individual from the forthcoming generation also possesses a predetermined life purpose to alleviate the psychological distress associated with apprehensions of both failure and success. Therefore, whenever they are on the brink of attaining substantial achievement, there arises a sensation of anticipation and apprehension as to their ability to endure and maintain this level of success, does it not?

To sum it up:
We exist as immortal entities existing within distinct physical vessels across various lifetimes, engaging with diverse genetic compositions. Nonetheless, our ultimate purpose remains singular: the progression of our souls. Therefore, the primary objective of engaging in meditation is to attain a state of unity in which we solely observe all the various experiences emanating from the multiple facets of our being. The preceding elucidation was provided solely to offer a glimpse into our existence as beings on a macro-level, and to emphasize the numerous facets in

which we must assume the role of a tacit observer during the practice of meditation. Regardless of discussing the shared collective consciousness encoded in our DNA or deliberating upon our previous life encounters, and even considering our present life experiences, ultimately, it is imperative to rid ourselves of the extraneous distractions in order to attain a state of wholeness and fulfillment once more.

Subsequent sections in this book shall present to you various modalities of meditation suited for different levels of our being, aiming to encompass every aspect, disentangle disturbances, and facilitate a harmonious alignment with the all-encompassing cosmic forces.

Posture For Meditation: A 7-Step Guide

In the context of Tibetan Buddhism, the utilization of the seven points of Vairocana serves as an effective means to engage in meditation. Allow me to present a method for engaging in meditation through the utilization of the 7 point meditation posture, which facilitates the cultivation of mindfulness, acceptance, and wisdom within oneself.

First point of body positioning: Take a seat

The primary and fundamental action is assuming a seated position on the terrain. This may appear disconcerting or unfamiliar to you, particularly if you are accustomed to sitting in a chair. However, after a few attempts, you gradually acclimate to this adjustment.

There exist various postural variations that one may experiment with in order to assume a comfortable sitting position on the ground, thereby enhancing one's ability to engage in effective meditation. You have the option to select the one that best aligns with your preferences.

Prior to proceeding with the selection of a posture, novice practitioners should emphasize the significance of establishing an appropriate meditation space. The location in which one engages in meditation undoubtedly holds great significance in shaping and influencing their level of concentration during the practice. In the event that you choose to engage in meditation within an environment characterized by excessive noise, it is highly probable that you will encounter considerable difficulty in maintaining a concentrated focus on the task at hand, thereby experiencing frequent disruptions in your ability to sustain attention.

It is imperative that the space in which you choose to meditate is thoroughly sanitized, systematically arranged, and devoid of any objects that may cause disorder. An untidy and disorganized environment poses numerous distractions. It is probable that your attention will be drawn to any object causing disorder in the surroundings, or you may experience discomfort due to the untidiness in the vicinity, or feel overwhelmed as soon as you occupy that position. Therefore, select a location for meditation that is hygienic, orderly, serene, and free from any potential sources of distraction.

It may be a secluded corner within your residence, a dedicated chamber, a serene location amidst the garden, or even within the confines of your vehicle; the crucial aspect is to engage in meditation within a space that fosters relaxation and heightened concentration. Please ensure the spot is clean, and, if you would be so kind, adorn it with any object or item that brings solace and facilitates a connection with your spiritual essence. Possible rephrasing in a formal tone: "It may consist of a diminutive Buddha sculpture, a decorative vessel for flowers, or any other object that facilitates the cultivation of tranquility."

Furthermore, it is crucial to select an appropriate posture for engaging in meditation. Regardless of the pose you decide upon, it is advisable to acquire a high-quality zafu, a specialized round cushion designed explicitly to facilitate comfortable and grounded meditation in any chosen pose while promoting effective mindfulness practice.

Nevertheless, in the event that you are disinclined to engage in such financial commitments at present, we suggest procuring either a pliable or sturdy cushion to facilitate a comfortable seated position on the floor. If you are capable of practicing this technique for a duration of 2 to 5 minutes initially, it is possible for you to find a comfortable position even without the aid of a cushion.

There exist six postures to adopt in order to engage in proper meditation according to the seven-point framework of Buddhist meditation.

The Sitting Pose with Crossed Legs

Unroll your yoga mat onto the floor and position your zafu or alternative cushion on top of it. Please assume a seated position with legs crossed, ensuring that both feet are comfortably positioned directly below the opposite knee or thigh. This particular pose is highly recommended and accessible for novice practitioners, given its remarkable simplicity and the absence of any unnecessary strain on one's body.

Half Lotus

This particular pose presents a more accessible adaptation of the complete lotus pose. If the quarter lotus pose presents excessive difficulty, refrain from situating both feet on the opposing thighs. Rather than simply crossing your legs, you may opt to elegantly place one foot on the opposite thigh or leg. One may opt to tuck their other foot beneath their upper leg, or alternatively, allow it to rest just below the thigh or knee.

Full Lotus Pose

This could be considered the optimal posture for achieving utmost stability throughout the practice and upholding a heightened level of concentration. Nevertheless, due to its somewhat challenging nature in terms of maintenance, a significant number of individuals encounter difficulty when attempting to perform the complete lotus pose, often opting for the half or quarter lotus variations initially.

To engage in this exercise, assume a comfortable seated position either on a zafu cushion or directly on the floor, and proceed to cross your legs with both feet resting comfortably upon the opposite thigh.

Burmese Pose

If assuming a seated position on the floor with legs in a crossed arrangement proves challenging, it is unnecessary to exert excessive effort in persevering with that posture. In due course, you will achieve the necessary stability, concentration, and adaptability required for proficiently mastering various lotus poses. However, in the interim, you may attempt the uncomplicated Burmese pose.

Assume a comfortable seated position with both feet resting firmly on the floor in the relaxed posture. For accomplishing this task with convenience, it is advised to procure a thick blanket which can be folded accordingly. Moreover, an alternate option that can be pursued involves utilizing a zafu or any other cushion with a firm composition as a suitable seat. Assume a seated position at the edge of the blanket or zafu, subsequently stretching your legs forward to extend them onto the ground for a stretching effect.

Please place one shin atop the other and proceed to gently separate both knees. Carefully slide your feet under the knees that are on the opposite side, and fold your legs inward towards your abdomen. Gently place your feet in a relaxed position, ensuring that the edges remain in contact with the floor and that the inner arches are positioned just below the opposing shins.

Seiza Pose

If assuming the Burmese posture proves to be challenging or causes discomfort, an alternative approach involves kneeling on the floor and placing a cushion between the legs in order to achieve a stable position.

Chair Pose

If none of the aforementioned positions prove suitable, particularly due to the initial difficulty beginners may encounter in sustaining them for even short durations, I recommend attempting the straightforward chair pose as an alternative. This merely entails assuming a seated position as opposed to engaging in any postural activity on the floor. There is no justification for feeling any sense of disgrace in utilizing a chair when necessary. If you are new to the practice of meditation, or if you have prior experience but are desirous of utilizing a chair, please feel free to do so without hesitation.

Meditation is a practice that embraces all aspects; it does not impose limitations on your actions or hinder your self-expression. Therefore, if you find it more suitable to sit on a chair during meditation, feel free to do so, as only when you are properly settled will you be able to meditate with the highest level of concentration. Please select any chair that suits your comfort and settle into it with ease. Please ensure that you maintain proper posture by refraining from slouching and ensuring that both of your feet remain firmly grounded. It is important to align your feet with your knees and hips.

In the event that none of these poses prove suitable for your initial attempts, you also have the option to recline on the floor for meditation. One drawback of reclining and engaging in meditation is that it frequently induces such a profound state of relaxation that one might inadvertently fall asleep. If you desire to assume a reclining position while engaging in meditation, kindly recline upon the exercise mat and position your knees upwards, while keeping your feet grounded on the floor. This imparts a state of alertness, thereby enabling one to remain consciously awake throughout the meditative practice.

It is advisable to experiment with each of these poses individually before proceeding with the actual practice in order to ascertain which ones are most suitable for you. Select the option that provides you with the utmost level of comfort and proceed to engage in deliberate practice. After assuming an appropriate stance, proceed to address the subsequent aspects of the position. The subsequent section provides in-depth explanations of these concepts.

An Analysis Of The Fundamental Aspects Of Meditation: The Elements Of Who, What, Where, When, Why, With, And How

Who discovered meditation?

Although it is challenging to ascertain an exact date for the emergence of meditation, it can be surmised that its origins can be traced back to numerous countries such as India, China, Japan, and Israel, among others, dating back several centuries. Our knowledge on this matter has primarily been derived from depictions of meditative postures in wall art and the interpretation of ancient texts. It is plausible that it originated during the early stages of human civilization. It has undergone substantial transformations and advancements over the course of centuries and continues to evolve in the contemporary world.

Certainly, meditation has undergone a process of development and has acquired clear definitions and structured practices, as is characteristic of human nature. Therefore, a plethora of meditation styles and types are available for selection in contemporary times.

Who meditates?

In accordance with a broad interpretation of meditation, individuals who immerse themselves deeply in their artistic, musical, intellectual, or creative endeavors, thereby attaining heightened concentration and attunement with spirituality, could be considered participants in the act of meditation. I hold the belief that individuals who derive satisfaction from taking walks or engaging in jogging amidst natural surroundings have the capacity to achieve a meditative state.

Numerous individuals aspire to enhance their self-awareness and spiritual consciousness amidst the backdrop of an industrialized and technologically advanced society. We inhabit a fast-paced realm where we encounter substantial levels of stress, anxiety, apprehension, sleep disturbances, hypertension, and a host of additional afflictions. Meditation, therefore, has been an integral aspect of existence for numerous individuals, dating back to the earliest stages of human cognition and the pursuit of self-understanding and transcendence.

Practitioners of meditation encompass individuals from diverse backgrounds, akin to individuals such as yourself and me. Typical instances of individuals who practice meditation encompass Buddhists, individuals in creative and artistic professions, musicians, mentors in personal development, executives in the corporate world, practitioners of yoga, figures in positions of global leadership, members of religious institutions such as churches and mosques, medical practitioners, scientists, actors, athletes, facilitators of vision board and life coaching sessions, parents, and even children as young as three years old.

Who can meditate?

The answer is anyone. A significant number of individuals across the globe opt for the practice of meditation. One may commence at any age. Meditation embraces humanity. Individuals who engage in the practice of meditation seek deliverance from various external and internal stimuli that give rise to cognitive, affective, spiritual, and somatic distress. It is utilized by individuals in pursuit of spiritual enlightenment and self-realization.

A considerable number of individuals remain oblivious to the fact that they are participating in daily meditation. Artisans engage in a state of deep reflection during the process of their artistic creation, vocalists and instrumentalists enter a contemplative state while performing, authors enter a state of introspection while penning their words, medical professionals engage in a focused state of concentration during surgical procedures, and explorers immerse themselves in a reflective state while traversing natural landscapes. Through the practice of individuals such as yourself and me, who engage in a personal connection with the natural world through the act of taking a walk.

Based on my past encounters, I have observed a recurring practice among individuals in the business community, which involves engaging in structured meditation. All of my business mentors advocate the incorporation of a variety of meditation practices into their daily routines. My personal coach and mentor diligently incorporates meditation into his daily morning routine. Oprah Winfrey, Michael Jordan, Katie Perry, LeBron James, Madonna, and Paul McCartney are a handful of prominent individuals belonging to the spheres of art, sports, and celebrity who openly declare their regular engagement in the practice of meditation. The daily practice of meditation is embraced by esteemed individuals such as Jack Dorsey, Twitter's CEO, Jeff Weiner, CEO of Linkedin, and Bill Gates, co-founder of Microsoft. It is noteworthy that these accomplished individuals attribute a portion of their achievements to their regular engagement in meditation.

Consequently, I strongly advocate for the practice of daily meditation as a means to enhance one's overall quality of life. Indeed, it is permissible to engage in a leisurely stroll while in a state of deep contemplation, or alternately, one can actively partake in a structured meditation practice aimed at attaining spiritual enlightenment. Ensure consistent daily practice.

I engage in deliberate meditation to alleviate mental strain stemming from daily pressures. The remainder of the advantages are inherent. For individuals who are new to meditation, the practice may evoke an initial sense of unfamiliarity once they begin contemplating its potential benefits, compelling them to cultivate a greater sense of spiritual consciousness. One might be curious as to how contemplating empty thoughts contributes to the resolution of emotional and physical ailments that one may be experiencing. And in the case of individuals with busy schedules, how can the act of engaging in idleness and abstaining from contemplation possibly provide any beneficial outcomes? Given your busy schedule, it is indeed a fact that one can engage in meditation. It will not impede your progress; rather, it will enhance your productivity!

I understand that this may seem unconventional, but I urge you to observe your surroundings. You will witness individuals from diverse backgrounds actively participating in this seemingly contradictory mode of living, embracing meditation as an essential element of their fruitful and wellness-oriented way of life.

WHAT

What is meditation?

In essence, it can be reiterated that meditation serves as a cerebral practice employed by individuals in order to attain an elevated level of spiritual consciousness.

Furthermore, it is imperative to acquire and diligently cultivate this competency on a daily basis, acknowledging that absolute perfection may still remain elusive despite one's efforts. Be easy on yourself. There may be occasions when you experience a sense of diversion. That access to it is denied. Your inability to maintain focus. No problem, no judgement.

What is my precise interpretation of the concept of meditation?

It is the place where my thoughts transcend, evoking a profound sense of connectedness with the Universe, particularly with the revered entity of Mother Earth. In moments devoid of any responsibilities, I am able to solely reside in the present moment. Upon the completion of my meditation practice, I experience a state of emotional tranquility and a heightened sense of physical energy, enabling me to approach the various obstacles of life with enhanced confidence and graceful composure.

According to the findings of various studies, it has been observed that artists engage in a state of unconscious meditation during the execution of their artistic endeavors, regardless of their specific medium or discipline. Engaging in repetitive expressions of gratitude, much like the renowned German physicist Albert Einstein, can be viewed as an alternate method of practicing meditation.

There exists a myriad of meditation techniques. I will enumerate ten of them, all of which I have employed during the process of locating the one that most suitably aligns with my lifestyle and the workshops conducted for my vision board initiative.

Novice individuals might find it worthwhile to engage in the practice of each technique, as they are notably uncomplicated to execute and comprehend. In the event of a demanding schedule, they will not excessively demand your time.

What attire is appropriate for meditation?

Comfort is a must. It is advised to don attire that is relaxed in fit and ensures optimal comfort. Select attire that promotes relaxation, alleviating the need to concern oneself with garments that are tight or constricting. You have the option to perform the task without footwear, or alternatively, you may choose to wear socks in conjunction with comfortable footwear.

However, if you opt to practice meditation in your office while wearing your professional attire, this suggestion may be disregarded. It is imperative that you dress in accordance with both your personal comfort and the prevailing norms of the environment in which you find yourself.

WHERE

Where does one meditate?

The most stylish response would be: within your thoughts. Transport your thoughts to a physical setting in which you ascertain optimal comfort and an environment conducive to relaxation, as well as a state of harmonious connection.

First and foremost, it is imperative to engage in meditation wherever possible. I am inclined to personally diversify my activities. I engage in daily meditation sessions on my veranda with a sweeping vista of the ocean, shortly before commencing my professional obligations. I consume 500 milliliters of water immediately upon awakening. Additionally, I ensure that I have a cup of coffee conveniently positioned beside me as I am consistently occupied and favor the portable option.

Can you kindly inform me about the most suitable location for me to engage in meditation?

Positioned above the ocean, amidst the forest, or atop my deck with views encompassing both of these breathtaking landscapes. Occasionally, I engage in the practice of visiting the seaside and engaging in contemplation upon a wooden trunk. I greatly derive pleasure from the auditory sensations evoked by the calls of seagulls and eagles, the resonating sound of the ferry's horn, and the rhythmic motion of waves gently caressing the shoreline. The aroma emanating from the sea evokes within me a sense of harmonious interconnectedness with the vastness of the cosmos.

I derive great pleasure from the forest as well. When I engage in contemplation amidst the trees, it becomes an ideal location. I perceive the melodious songs of birds and the gentle rustling of leaves. I perceive the aroma of coniferous trees, the soil, and blooming flora. Additionally, it is an ethereal location where I can walk upon the sacred ground barefoot, connected to the Earth.

What is the location you consider to be your ideal spot?

An environment characterized by tranquility and devoid of auditory disturbances or potential interruptions may be preferable to you. It is permissible to experience auditory stimuli that establish a connection with the natural environment. I do not have any objection to the presence of natural sounds, such as the gentle breeze causing the leaves to rustle, the melodious songs of birds, or the soothing sound of ocean waves upon the shore. Certain individuals prefer to have calming or therapeutic music gently resonating within the ambient surroundings of a particular space. This approach proves to be highly effective during my vision board workshops.

If it is within your capacity to maintain a proper seated posture, we encourage you to do so for as long as you find it agreeable. If you are solely capable of assuming a reclined position, then adopt this method. I can provide you with my assurance that it will yield the same outcome.

If you find yourself situated within a hospital chamber, that shall suffice as well. If you find yourself standing atop a mountain, take pleasure in the experience. If you find yourself traveling on public transportation such as a bus or train during your daily commute, or if you are situated in an office setting enclosed within a cubicle, then by all means, proceed. If you happen to find yourself in an elevator malfunctioning, it presents an opportune situation.

I am aware that eventually, all forms of diversions will fade from the realm of your thoughts as enlightenment assumes dominance, rendering the location of your meditation inconsequential. I am aware of a six-year-old child who frequents a daycare facility and, in instances where he experiences mild unease, effectively communicates his discomfort to his caregiver and subsequently relocates to a different area of the room, away from the hubbub of other boisterous children, in order to engage in meditative practices. No problem.

Please trust my assertion that as a novice in this time-honored practice, you will derive great pleasure from exploring the myriad of locations available for your meditation endeavors. It will broaden your perspective and allow you to immerse yourself in the myriad benefits that a meditation-focused lifestyle can bring. Your life will undergo a permanent transformation. Wherever you may venture, be it with intention or without, you shall continuously and instinctively seek out a space in which to engage in the practice of meditation. With regards to individuals who are occupied with various commitments, what are your thoughts? The same principles also hold true.

WHEN

You have the freedom to engage in meditation at any time that suits you. Certain experts may refer to your synchronicity with celestial bodies or the optimal timing during the day when your cognitive clarity is heightened. That, I would not be. My mental faculties remain ceaselessly engaged, commencing at daybreak and subsiding come nightfall. I am currently experiencing a significant improvement in my well-being and have attained a higher level of relaxation. I am a firm advocate of regular meditation.

I often engage in morning meditation due to the observation that upon awakening, I experience tension in my shoulders and find my mind preoccupied with various thoughts and concerns. My mind was already spinning in circles. I would suggest incorporating mornings into your daily routine, as it serves as an excellent way to commence the day.

During the middle of the day, I allocate a ten-minute period for meditation to recharge my energy levels, which often become depleted as a result of my work responsibilities by the time lunch hour arrives. Meditation is imperative in the evening for me as it allows me to relinquish the demands of another arduous eight (or more) hours of work. It provides me with a restful night's sleep, free from any unsettling thoughts. I have a predilection for solitary meditation, typically engaging in three sessions per day, although occasionally I experience an inclination to engage in additional practice.

Identify the optimal period within each day for engaging in meditation. In a designated setting of your preference, whether accompanied or in solitude, please proceed at your own pace. It constitutes a journey of self-exploration that will bestow lifelong benefits upon you.

Should you find yourself occupied, it shan't be long before you witness the advantages, prompting you to effortlessly allocate additional moments daily for the practice of meditation. It will alleviate your work-related emotional distress and revitalize your well-being. That will serve as your motivation to allocate time for it in subsequent occasions.

Busy individuals may opt for the workplace due to its tendency to induce high levels of anxiety, stress, and exhaustion. Practicing mindfulness in the workplace has been found to have a positive impact on stress indicators, diminish feelings of irritability, and enhance both productivity and the capacity to concentrate. Additionally, it has been shown to bolster energy levels. Given that the majority of individuals allocate a significant portion of their daily routines to office-related engagements, it stands as an opportune setting for incorporating such an activity into one's schedule.

Regarding novices, the timing of meditation will depend on your acquisition of the techniques necessary for its practice. It may be advisable to schedule specific time slots, ideally two to three times a day, during which you can engage in a brief period of guided meditation.

WHY

Due to the plethora of advantages that meditation offers, certain repercussions thereof can be observed promptly. There exist numerous compelling justifications for the practice of meditation, a selection of which I have delineated within the title of my book.

I have compiled a comprehensive collection of compelling justifications that may incite your interest in the exploration of meditation at present. Please be advised that there is no cost associated with this activity.

Benefits of meditation

1.

Reduces stress

2.

Reduces anxiety

3.

Mitigates anxiety through cognitive redirection.

4.

Promotes psychological and emotional well-being
5.
May enhance your libido
6.
Reduces memory loss
7.
Helps fight addictions
8.
Results in favorable outcomes and appreciation.
9.
Inspires forgiveness
10.
Supports sleep health
11.
Reduces pain
12.
Helps control blood pressure
13.
Leads to spiritual awareness
14.
Enhances your concentration at work and on the present tasks.
15.
Increases your attention span
16.

Facilitates a strong mind-body connection

17. Enhances your perception of existence "

18. Aids in establishing a greater sense of stability and centeredness.

19. Alters your responses to internal and external conflicts

20. Increases your self-awareness

21. Enhances individuals' capacity to demonstrate empathy and compassion towards others.

22. Enhances the sense of liberation

23. Eradicates negative thoughts

24. Eliminates mental barriers or impediments.

25. Awakens happiness

Prior to commencing the practice of meditation, ascertain the underlying purpose or motivation behind your engagement. What is the rationale behind your desire to partake in meditation? What benefits or advantages do you stand to gain from this? Examine the list of advantages and ascertain whether any one of them or multiple ones would serve as a suitable source of motivation. Please take notes if necessary.

Might it be due to the presence of stress that you are experiencing such emotions? That constituted my foremost motive in commencing. I incessantly harbored concerns about virtually every aspect of my life, leading me to adopt a melodramatic attitude, experience extreme agitation, engage in behaviors that undermined my own success, and ultimately caused a spike in my blood pressure. Consequently, I experienced discontent.

Another factor that motivated me to start was the abundance of individuals I encountered who engage in meditation, exuding profound contentment and tranquility. They manifest appreciation, exhibit empathy, and exhibit a lack of excessive distress. Thus, the fundamental inquiry becomes, what rationale exists against practicing meditation? Why not pursue self-awareness and enlightenment in light of the inherent unpredictability and demands of our current world? Why not engage in mental escapism and devote a few moments every day to simply exist?

As a novice in the practice of meditation, your exploration of the reasons behind your interest could lead to a captivating voyage of self-improvement, enabling you to discern your emotions and determine your responses to the tumultuous events unfolding in your surroundings.

The rationale behind the mindset of individuals who are busy can potentially be rooted in their desire to enhance their way of life, thus alleviating the perpetual feeling of busyness. Being occupied typically indicates experiencing stress, anxiety, a sense of urgency, and striving to meet unattainable deadlines and professional performance standards. They, too, will learn to choose how they will react to stress. Why not endeavor to enhance one's standard of living? You are deserving of it, considering all the circumstances.

www.ingramcontent.com/pod-product-compliance
Lightning Source LLC
Chambersburg PA
CBHW050419120526
44590CB00015B/2025